A Prayer for Millennials

A Prayer for Millennials

The Spiritual Journey of a Millennial Adventurer

Gabriel Picazo

RESOURCE *Publications* · Eugene, Oregon

A PRAYER FOR MILLENNIALS
The Spiritual Journey of a Millennial Adventurer

Resource Publications
An Imprint of Wipf and Stock Publishers
199 W. 8th Ave., Suite 3
Eugene, OR 97401

www.wipfandstock.com

PAPERBACK ISBN: 979-8-3852-6042-3
HARDCOVER ISBN: 979-8-3852-6043-0
EBOOK ISBN: 979-8-3852-6044-7

VERSION NUMBER 11/06/25

To Esther, my mother, "The Island"

and to Catarina, my luna, "The Soulmate."

Contents

Acknowledgments | ix
Author's Note | xi
Introduction | xiii

The Island | 1
The Diver | 7
The Academy | 12
The Artist | 18
The Aviator | 26
The Soulmate | 38
My Generation | 53
A Need for Something Real | 58

Epilogue | 67
Bibliography | 71

Acknowledgments

THIS BOOK WOULD NOT be in your hands today without the hard work, assistance, and loving guidance of Tracy Murphy, my editor. Thank you immensely for believing in my first book.

Author's Note

I WAS BORN ON the 3rd of June of the year 1995, which, when you think about it, is right in the middle of the year and right in the middle of the last decade of the millennium. With one foot in the 20th century and the other foot in the 21st, my generation is probably the best qualified to be truly called "Millennial." That being said, if you do your research, you will find that sources differ on where exactly the Millennial generation ends and Generation Z begins, leaving those of us born between 1994 and 1996 in somewhat of a limbo. Some of us feel too young to relate to a lot of "true" Millennial pop culture references, while at the same time, we are too old to be called "Gen Z."

The Spiritual Journey of a Millennial Adventurer is, by definition, a memoir. In the following pages, I tell the story of my young life as an adventurer, an aviator, a musician, a wanderer, a hopeless romantic, but most of all, a young person with a spiritual calling. You will find that this book is, at its core, a criticism of the ideologies from the modern world, particularly the ridiculous belief that we no longer need religion or spiritual practices in our lives.

I wrote this book with many friends, acquaintances, classmates, and young family members in mind. I wanted to find an artistic way of conveying to them this spiritual message while avoiding a face-to-face confrontation that might come off to them as old-fashioned, outdated, or "preachy." So while I originally intended this book for my fellow Millennials and Gen Zs, I soon realized that these issues affect everyone living in the 21st century. Many people from older generations can easily relate to the ideas I talk about here, and those from Generation Alpha and the generations to come will perhaps find this conversation even more relevant.

I sincerely hope that this book will work as an antidote against the epidemic of depression, anxiety, and the lack of meaning that our shallow modern ideologies leave behind. A reminder to put our faith in the things that faith belongs to, and to rely only on the timeless truths and the immortal essence of our human spirit.

Introduction

WHAT IS IT THAT makes your heart race?

I have always had an obsession with human passion and the things that people dedicate a lifetime to pursuing. How a chef can turn a simple task like eating into a work of art that melts into a thousand flavors on your palate. How, in the process of songwriting, a musician pulls from the ether, like a sorcerer conjuring up a creature from another dimension, a song he claims has always existed, "It just needed to be written down," they say.

Me? I have always strived for a life of adventure. To escape the nine-to-five and to avoid at all costs working a job in an office. This is probably thanks to the influence of my father (a scuba diver, musician, and traveler), whom I lost when I was fourteen. My father inspired me to live a life out of the ordinary, to explore new places often, and to never allow my life to turn into a monotonous routine.

Flying is probably the love of my life. I wanted to skydive since the moment I knew what a parachute was. I had my "baptism of the air" in an ultralight when I was seventeen, and I joined flight school at twenty. After that, I learned how to sail (who doesn't want to feel free like a pirate?) and got certified as a skipper. Years before that, I learned archery and tried my luck as a musician and writer of songs; nowadays. . . I'm looking into motorcycles, flying paragliders, and hunting with falcons.

Here is a little secret: As much as I love flying and these other adventurous activities, nothing makes me as happy as thinking about these:

That I, and the universe where I live, were made by a God who loves me and made with a purpose. That some things are meant to be, like my mother was meant to be my mother and no one else's, and that I was meant to find my soulmate and she was meant to find me and save me. And that after our time in this world is over. . . there's yet another adventure waiting for us.

I have always lived my life adhering to these beliefs and principles, even when many around me seemed to be completely indifferent to the spiritual. When I was a kid going to school, I didn't know how to talk about these things to my classmates and friends; perhaps I didn't fully believe in the importance of having that strong spiritual foundation that my parents spoke about, since I saw many of my friends living an apparently normal life in a secular household. Now. . . fast forward into the second decade of the 21st century, and I see so many of those same peers fighting a battle against anxiety, depression, and a meaningless existence, living in a confused world that openly denies the same sciences it once held as sacred. A world consumed by social media and social justice. A world where the arts wither and turn grey one by one, the same color as the minimalist buildings that surround us with soulless architecture, standing where once stood colorful temples and great cathedrals.

One could not have asked to be born in a better moment in history to prove atheism and secularism wrong. I believe this is the ultimate mission for my generation of millennials, and this is the spiritual journey of a millennial adventurer.

The Island

SOMEWHERE ON THE SOUTHEASTERN tip of Mexico, about ten kilometers from the mainland of Cancún, lies a little island rising from the Caribbean Sea. The island itself, no larger than seven kilometers, was discovered in the sixteenth century by the Spanish, who, upon arriving, saw only women inhabitants and named it "Isla Mujeres" (The Isle of Women), or so the legend goes. These days, Isla Mujeres is a famous stop for sailors venturing across the Caribbean. It is also home to native Mexicans, a few Americans who want to escape the 9-to-5 hustle culture, as well as a few Europeans fleeing harsh weather and ice-cold beaches.

By the time I was born in 1995, my dad had already traveled a big chunk of the world collecting stamps in his scuba dive logbook. By the time he was a certified instructor, he decided it was time for us to move out of the big city and live on an island to pursue his dream of starting a scuba diving business, thus beginning my lifelong quest for adventure, my love for motion, and my aversion to urban life.

Life on a small island is pretty much as you would imagine, and it definitely fits that "tight-knit" community stereotype that country singers write about. One time, my mother's cousin from the city thought it would be a great idea to surprise us with a visit. He flew all the way from Mexico City, jumped on the ferry, crossed to the island, and found our house just by asking around for my mother by name!

To be fair, my mom had built herself a bit of a reputation by then. Even though it was hard for her to fit in at the beginning (being quite the city girl that she was, getting dragged by a scuba diver/mariner to live on an island). A devout Catholic and incredibly kind-hearted, my mom has always had an instinct to protect the weak and help those in need. It's funny how things turn out in small communities. I believe that people are most likely to find their calling and reach their full potential when we are in small communities. "Everybody dies famous in a small town," or so they say. It is easy to feel like just another number when living in a big city, competing against thousands for a job, and getting lost in the crowd of unrecognizable faces on your everyday commute. In a small town, everybody knows you by name, or knows your face at least. You are not competing with others as much as you are working for the common good, and sometimes you might be the only one, or part of a select few, who can perform your specific trade. In the big city, you may be just another mechanic, but in a small town, you could be the only one who can fix the car of everyone's favorite newlywed couple before their honeymoon. Maybe humans were never meant to inhabit gigantic concrete wastelands and live among millions, don't you think?

The first few years adapting to the island were hard for my mom. It's hard to win the hearts of locals and integrate into an already established community, so when she kept getting rejected by every employer on the island, she turned to volunteer work.

Eventually, she was welcomed into "The Little Yellow School House" —a school for children with special needs—as a volunteer. She eventually became a teacher and finally made her way up to being named the school's principal. I am more than certain that in the big city, they would have had a thing or two to say to her had she chosen to take this turn in her career path over there. "But you don't have a degree to work as a teacher," or "You need a special certification on top of that if you wish to work with children with special needs," they would have said. There was nothing of the sort on our little island. My mom's accountancy degree was impressive enough for them, and they learned to appreciate her natural talents when it came to helping people. She would often get compliments from the school's psychologist when they read my mother's individual reports on the kids. They could not believe that she wasn't a licensed therapist. After a few years, my mom, who had once been an accountant in Mexico City, was now negotiating deals with Americans to bring in donations and materials for her school and socializing with the European socialites of the island.

She took her role as a guardian and protector of these children seriously. She would often continue working outside of school hours, driving to the houses of these kids, meeting their parents, and helping them understand how to care for them patiently and lovingly. She would even track down the parents accused of violent behavior towards their children—whether they were my mother's students or not—and try to intervene, to have a conversation with them, or to call the police if necessary.

I returned to the island over two decades later on a quest you will learn about towards the end of this book. I had visited a few times before, of course, but this time I made sure to pay a visit to the Little Yellow School. I was overwhelmed with emotion when I saw how much it had grown and how well it's been maintained. What was once a single building with a couple of classrooms now has two stories, a playground, a separate principal's office building, and even a café. It is fair to say that the place made me feel simply peaceful.

As I reminisced within its yellow walls, I couldn't help but appreciate all the fruits of my mom's labor. We often worry about leaving a mark and making an impact in this world before we move on to the next, but we often think of achieving it by becoming famous or going "viral," as millennials say. Seeing my mother's work made me realize that the impact we have on the world often has nothing to do with whether or not people know us; just as we are the living legacy of our ancestors, little does it matter if we don't know their names beyond two or three generations. Many new volunteers and teachers at the Little Yellow School today know nothing about my mom, but her impact and legacy are tangibly obvious in the very foundations of this place. It was a pleasant surprise when I was later greeted by name in the principal's office. While I was given a tour for the memories, the staff showed me photographs on the walls that told the story of the beginnings of this lovely institution. Sure enough, you can find me and my mom there, frozen in time, in the historical timeline of The Little Yellow School.

At only three years of age, I was mostly oblivious to the lifestyle changes one faces when moving to a different environment, so I adapted quickly to rural life. To me, everything revolved around my parents and my island friends. I was enrolled in kindergarten upon our arrival and later moved up to elementary school. It was a tiny island indeed, so the friends I made in kindergarten were in the same elementary school, and our friend group only got bigger.

These were the first real friends of my life, and their names were Erik, Sofía, Frida, and Lyra.

That last one became my first crush, or "first love," as they call it. I only later realized that she was the governor's daughter! Our elementary school was the only private school on the island at the time, so it figures the city boy would end up in school with the local "royalty."

I believe millennials are a generation that truly owns their name. We were born at the end of a millennium, just before the technological takeover. We had video games (GameCube, PlayStation 1, Game Boy) and computers (the big dinosaur-looking ones), even early mobile phones, but we still managed to have a childhood outdoors. We took turns going to friends' houses after school, played soccer on the streets, and had sword fights with sticks. Living so close to Mother Nature only made things better.

One time, my mom arranged for my friends and me to participate in a beautiful island tradition hosted by the local turtle museum. Every year, when turtle eggs hatch, volunteers (mostly kids) join forces to assist the baby turtles make their way to the sea. Kids put a newborn turtle in their tiny palms and carry them to the water, where it's happily released away from the dangers of land and air predators. Nothing beats the feeling of holding the life of a baby turtle in your palms, where you can feel its little flippers moving in excitement as they get closer and closer to the ocean!

I remember my mom and I picking up some of my friends and driving them to the event. I mostly remember pulling up on the driveway of Lyra's house and ringing the doorbell of what looked to me like Isla Mujeres' version of the White House. It must have looked like a six-year-old's version of the movie *My Date with the President's Daughter*.[1]

Releasing newborn turtles into the Caribbean Sea is quite the first date, don't you think? Perhaps this was my mom's way of teaching me how to be romantic for the future, for when I grew up and met the right girl . . .

There must be something about living surrounded by the ocean that made me hyperaware of the passage of time, even at an early age. The latitude or time zone, combined with the lack of modern distractions, made it feel like the sun was setting way too soon, too quickly after sunrise; this made me ponder questions of life and death, the soul, and the afterlife from an early age.

I don't know many second graders who spend entire summers asking their parents what happens when you die, but I feel like I did. I probably spent hours considering every possibility of the afterlife: from Heaven and reincarnation to complete oblivion. I remember asking God several times not to allow me to reincarnate, or if reincarnation was real, I always wanted my mom to be *my mom* in every single lifetime. "Please, please, please!"

By now, you probably get the idea that I am very fond of my mother. How could I not, if we spent so much time together on the island?

1. *My Date with the President's Daughter*. 1998. A teenage boy unwittingly falls for the American president's daughter, and the pair soon find themselves on a first-date adventure, dodging the Secret Service, trying to make it to a high school dance.

Most people think that my father was the greater influence in my life because I grew up to learn to fly airplanes and to travel the world. If that were so, this book would be a Kerouac-style adventure journal instead of the spiritual journey of a millennial boy.

I didn't get hurt many times playing while I was growing up; my wounds were more emotional, and my mom knew the right balm for every single one. She knew the balm for the fear of the unknown is the spiritual. The balm for too many questions is the search for Truth. The balm for insecurities is self-confidence. She even knew the balm for bullies at school: to show them kindness.

My mom has always known how to fight my fears, and when I was a kid, she went to great lengths to do so.

In the mornings when I was dreading the idea of going to school, my mom would get up earlier and drive me around the coast at sunrise so I had something beautiful to look at and something to look forward to. It felt like the drive to school was too quick, so she made it longer and scenic.

I suppose it is fair to say I was a little spoiled. "You're spoiling that kid!" everyone told my mom. "Better too much love than too much anger," she would reply.

My mom taught me many things that wouldn't fit in this book, and she continues to do so. But above all, she taught me faith. Not blind faith or fanatic faith, but true, spiritual, open-minded, and intellectual faith; one that walks side by side with reason. I would need this faith to draw strength from, to comfort me, and to guide me through the moral battlefield of growing up as a millennial kid in the 21st century.

The Diver

My father once told me that his first dream was to be an aviator and soar through the skies. However, one day, while wandering freely by the docks of some Mexican coast, he saw the most beautiful, brightly colored fish swimming in the crystal-clear water. That day, he fell in love with the ocean, or to be more precise, what's beneath the surface. Like Captain Nemo, my father's love was the submarine world, so he became a scuba diver.

I have always had a deep interest in people's passions; it's fascinating to put yourself in someone else's shoes and imagine what makes them so fond of cooking, designing a theater, or building an engine. It doesn't take much effort for me to understand my dad's love for the submarine world. After all, he raised me on an island. One of my favorite things to do while I was living there was swimming in the early evening with my mask and snorkel, exploring the small ecosystem beneath the docks. There was so much life there, from small fish to sea urchins and peculiar crabs crawling along the algae-covered wooden poles.

One of the most immersive experiences you can ever have is to do all this while it's raining in the world above the surface. If you take a mask and explore the world underwater while it's raining, you will discover that the submarine world is for the most part undisturbed. You will see the marine life going about their day with such comfort that you can't help but feel sheltered from the tempest above your head. The soothing sound of the raindrops colliding with the ocean is a plus, and the best part is going above the surface for a mouthful of air, and realizing you don't really care about the rain anyway because you're already wet! Then you submerge once more to seek shelter underwater and realize, if you're lucky, that now it's even warmer and cozier down there than above the surface.

It is safe to say my dad was an adventurer, a man of the sea, and quite a master in his field. My mother can tell you stories of how he would predict hurricanes just by feeling the temperature at a certain depth or watching the currents while scuba diving. Once, he was abandoned by his boat crew while diving in the middle of the ocean, right between Cancún and Isla Mujeres. When he didn't return home by sunset, my mom called the authorities, who sent an unsuccessful search and rescue operation. My dad had to ditch his gear, save for the flippers and mask, and swim all the way back to the island. Once he reached the shore, he still had to walk home because no taxi would pick up a wet diver!

Even to this day, I still meet people who share whole new stories of his adventures. There's always some distant cousin I haven't met or an uncle I haven't seen in ages telling me how my dad took them on their first scuba dive, or taught them how to backpack across Europe, or how they saw him swimming with whale sharks.

My dad probably made many mistakes in his lifetime, having been raised by an abusive father himself and losing his mother during childbirth when he was only eight years old. Anyone with a troubled childhood like that is bound to make a chain of mistakes, but regardless of his flaws, he was a great father figure to me.

If I had to pick a single favorite thing about being a millennial—besides the fancy name—it would be how many of us were raised by Star Wars dads. I used to judge how cool my friends' parents were by whether they watched Star Wars together. The way they chose to release the second set of movies sixteen years after the first set resulted in the perfect generation-bonding movie experience. I watched the first three films countless times with my dad in our home on the island, and when the time came, we watched the new films together in the movie theater. It is safe to say I grew up with Jedi as my role models.

I lost my dad on a Saturday when I was fourteen. We lost him to that infamous disease that takes the lives of loved ones, you know the one.

I have to say I wasn't too worried for most of the time he spent sick. I was raised to have faith, and coming from a Catholic family with more than one doctor, I grew up hearing many stories of real miracles. Accounts of unexplainable recoveries from incurable diseases came from both close to home (my aunt and godmother, Veronica, the doctor) and from far away.

I was certain my dad would get better, either through the miracles of modern medicine or the miracles of supernatural forces.

I tell you all this so you can understand how shattered my heart was when they took me to the hospital to see him when he started getting worse. I wasn't allowed inside because I was a minor, so my mom arranged for me to wait in the courtyard, where I would have a line of sight to the window of his hospital room. My mom made the phone call, and I looked up to see my dad suddenly appear in a gown and hooked to an IV. He was waving his arms in a motion as if wielding an invisible sword, a lightsaber. . .

I understood the message immediately; it was a reference to our conversations where we agreed he was going to use "The Force" (Star Wars' version of God) to beat his disease and get better.

To this day, I don't know what clicked in me at that moment. It was a combination of how well my dad and I knew each other to the point where a single wave of arms in a swordsman's posture could carry so much meaning. Seeing him in the hospital clothes, so close yet so far away from me. . . separated by a window.

Whatever it was that "clicked" made me break down in tears like I had never cried before or after. I was crying my eyes out in the backseat during the entire drive home, which, in city traffic, took probably over an hour. Somewhere in that car ride, I must have figured out that there was almost no chance that he would get better.

We lost my dad on a Saturday morning.

As luck would have it, I later saw more than one of my close friends or relatives lose their fathers at almost the same age, and in two cases, to the same disease. This is the point where many lost their faith in miracles, if not in God completely. And this is not an event exclusive to my generation.

I think that to stop believing in miracles because one didn't happen to you is like getting mad at your favorite singer for not spotting you in the crowd and going out of his way to sign your t-shirt.

There is a reason why the word "miracle" is synonymous with "uncommon." Even in Scripture, God makes people work really hard when they want one, but this doesn't mean that miracles aren't real. It would take a gigantic book to record all the best reports of miracles, especially the ones where scientists or doctors witnessed the events and confirmed that there was no possible scientific explanation. From the recent case of Tammy Peterson (wife of my favorite psychologist, Dr. Jordan Peterson) getting cured from a late-stage terminal disease in Canada after praying with a rosary blessed by the Pope, to the miracles of people who bathe in the waters of Lourdes, France.

If I had all the money in the world, I would pay someone to compile such a book of miracles, then gather the world's most famous atheists and skeptics and pay them to get on a stage and try to dissect and debunk each and every one. They would only get to page three or four before the audience realized how ridiculous they sounded.

"Maybe there was something in the weather that day" or "Oh, she must have eaten some very good apple that morning that cured her stage four cancer."

Another thing that is extremely unhelpful and makes young people lose their faith when they lose someone they love is when someone tries to comfort them, saying, "It was God's plan" or "God willed it for a reason."

I have learned that when theologians and religious figures talk about "God's plan," they mostly mean cosmic events that take billions of years to happen and how it all ties together with human history; in other words, the big picture and how we fit into it. They don't mean that you bumped your head against the wall this morning because God willed it.

I will share this in my mother's words, so she becomes like your mother too while you read my book, if it comforts you . . .

"God is love, and God is life. He is not death or disease. These things are not of Him, nor does He will them or give them to people. These are only things of the world in which we inhabit."

On the day he passed, one of his brothers told me what seemed to me the only words in the world that can truly comfort a person at a time like this:

"Now he is always going to be with you."

The diver had turned into a guardian angel.

Even to this day, it is extremely rare for me to really miss my father or wish he could still be walking among the living. Why would I wish for a butterfly to go back to the chrysalis?

I always feel him with me. Sometimes he's as close as being right next to me when I'm in the ocean or at the controls of an airplane. I talk to my father almost every day, telling him about my day, my dreams, and my hopes. Sometimes it feels just like talking to him face-to-face; other times, it feels like a telephone line, where the reception is sometimes good, other times poor. But I always know he is listening with a smile.

The Academy

AFTER SEVEN YEARS LIVING on the island and one more on the coast of Cancún, the powers that be decided that it was time to go back to Mexico City. My father was still with us at the time and would be for another four years. After his passing, our days of nomadic lifestyle would come to a prolonged pause. There, in the academies of the big city, is where I completed most of my education.

I can say in all honesty that the whole six years of my elementary education, as well as another three of middle school, were perfectly normal and free of ideological indoctrination. Due to our travels, I did those nine years in four different schools; only one of them was a Catholic academy (La Salle), and the other three were regular secular schools spread around Isla Mujeres, Cancún, and Mexico City. I enjoyed my time in all of them as much as a bird can enjoy its time in a comfortable and elegant cage. It is no surprise that kids don't like school, so you can imagine how a kid who grows up to learn how to fly an airplane feels about sitting all day at a desk in school. Still, I was able to enjoy a normal education free from any ideological agendas; this would change radically once I was enrolled in high school. The truth is that I got to experience early on what the "college environment" was like for my generation, because I attended a high school that was connected to the university

I planned to go to after graduation. So, at fifteen years old, I was thrown into the pit of liberal academia.

As soon as I started walking those halls, I felt uncomfortable, but at the time I was too young and uneducated to understand why. It took me years to put a finger on it: I was witnessing the first stages of a "mind virus" that would take over Western academia in the next decade.

Anarchy symbols were always present in the dark corners of those campuses; later in my university, they were accompanied by the hammer and sickle flags of the communist party hanging from almost every building on the campus. Soon, most of my classmates started reading books like *Animal Farm* by George Orwell and *The Communist Manifesto* by Karl Marx. Most professors seemed to endorse these ideologies, while those who disagreed didn't speak up often enough.

This environment left little room for spirituality or for the theological conversations that once lit the hearts of academics. My contemporaries constantly antagonized religion, fueled by their Marx-leaning political ideologies and Nietzsche-inspired philosophies.

My spirituality was never truly in conflict with academia before this point. Perhaps as a child, I felt uneasy in science class when we talked about things like the origin of the universe and the plausible scientific explanations. But I was raised Catholic, not in a fundamentalist-televangelist sect like the ones I will discuss later. If that were the case, I might have ended up as an atheist.

I soon learned about the beautiful relationship between faith and reason, and between religion and science. The Big Bang Theory is often mentioned in class, for example, but not everyone knows it was first conceived by a Catholic priest who was also a physicist.

There is a wonderful article called "What the Church Has Given the World"[1] by Fr. Marcus Holden and Fr. Andrew

1. Pinsent and Holden, *What the Church has given the world.*

Pinsent—another physicist/priest, funny enough. They detail the long-existing relationship between the Church and science, going from the foundations of genetics and geology to the basic principles of law, music theory, and even women's rights.

The challenge I faced in high school and university was different. Like modern advocates of the "New Atheism" movement, the Marx-indoctrinated staff at my university argued that religion is detrimental to civilization. I remember an argument I started once in the middle of a film theory lecture because my professor was upset about the Mexican founding fathers' decision to have the white color of the Mexican flag represent the Catholic faith. "We started this country on the wrong foot!" he cried.

In these situations, my mother came to the rescue yet again. While I navigated these years of higher education, she enrolled in a four-year theology program, solely motivated by her desire to answer the complicated questions her son often asked on a spiritual journey. She learned much about apologetics and told me all about it on our drives home from school or over breakfast in some cozy restaurant on the weekends. Through her, I would learn some basics of theology. I now had tools to defend Christianity, Judaism, Hinduism, or any other formal religion against the attacks of my Nietzsche-brainwashed peers.

What an ignorant remark my film theory professor made; I think of him every time I watch a new video or speech from prominent atheists. They used to claim, in essence, that religion and spiritual practice are false, of course, but since their movement didn't achieve anything tangible and permanent in decades, they moved to the more radical idea that faith and religion are not only false but evil, setting a goal to eradicate them from the world.

"Religion causes wars," they say. "Faith kills people. Look at the Inquisition, look at terrorist attacks!"

These examples expose their flawed logic. The first one falls into what I like to call anachronistic judgment. Think of a genuine war or a violent movement solely started because of religion. Chances are, you are thinking of some time period where people were wearing metal armor and relying on horses for transportation. People were killing people for all sorts of ridiculous reasons back in those days, religion being just one of them. Saying that this is still a problem in the 21st century is not only a stretch, but it also means claiming that we haven't evolved at all, that we haven't grown and learned from our mistakes as human beings.

The second example addresses contemporary issues like terrorist attacks, but if religion turns people into terrorists, why isn't every spiritual person one?

The leading voices of the "new atheist" movement are genuinely intelligent people, usually with high IQs, so it amuses me how they fail to see that religion, faith, and spiritual practice aren't the cause of violence; ignorance and fanaticism are.

People who live in ignorance are always at risk of becoming extreme fanatics—not only of religion, but of anything at all. Some people have even been killed in the modern era in heated confrontations between fans of opposing soccer teams. Atheists don't advocate for education or tolerance; instead, they advocate for eliminating soccer completely.

There are some who say that our Western civilization is a flower rooted in religious values and traditions; once you cut the flower and wave it around, it will only last so long before showing signs of withering.

I have to say I was lucky enough to witness only the very first waves of ¨woke culture¨ and gender ideology during my academic studies; they only came during the very last years of my time in university, but like the flower withering, I saw the signs coming from miles away.

I remember the first few times that I had to sit and listen to some of my classmates give us a presentation about the new "revolutionary ideas" in the field of "gender theory." They argued that gender was a social construct and anybody could pick whatever gender they chose to be, and now they expected us to believe there were more than two. I couldn't believe my eyes as I looked around and saw everyone listening and nodding with straight faces; even more so, I just couldn't believe that the professors were doing nothing about it and going along with it with no questions.

"Everyone is free to express their opinions," I thought. "But this is like saying the Earth is flat, and we're supposed to be in a university!"

To some, it may seem a stretch to conclude that the lack of religious values and traditions alone is a major reason why the "woke mind virus"—as I call it—was allowed to infiltrate the world of academia. Many people still believe that reason (academia) and faith (religion) are incompatible, but it is essential to remember that religious institutions also played a foundational role in the academic world. Yet another fact that is easily overlooked by my generation is that the entire university system was developed by the Catholic Church! Many of the greatest universities, such as Oxford and Cambridge, were established by the Church.

Even my alma mater, the National Autonomous University of Mexico, where my cranky anti-religious professor still teaches, is considered the historical and spiritual successor to the Pontifical University of Mexico.

It is funny but not surprising that almost the only people immune to the brainwashing effects of "woke culture" when it first started were intellectual, religious people. Look at the most celebrated "anti-woke" speakers of today; some are recent "converts" who found their faith precisely because it seemed to them like the only escape from all this modern ideological confusion; famous actor and comedian Russell Brand is a great example. But most of the speakers against gender ideology early on were, and still are, deeply religious people.

Nowadays, even many atheists have joined in the fight against gender ideology. This is because atheists hold reason as sacred—ironically so—and the "gender-ideology agenda" poses the biggest threat to reason and science that our world has seen in many centuries.

This probably wasn't the case, though, during the 20th century, when Alfred Kinsey, with his depraved sexual research experiments, and John Money, with his theory that gender could be socially determined after birth, caught the attention of the academic world and planted the seeds of gender ideology. I wasn't around at the time, and there aren't many records of public opinion back then, but I am willing to bet that most atheists supported both "mad scientists" when they were paving the way to rid society of its traditional Judeo-Christian sexual values. That is not a dig at the atheist movement for turning against this madness. It is, after all, only the wise who can change their minds.

Still, it seems that for centuries, religious values have served as an "early warning system" hidden in our subconscious, alerting us when a new ideology that seemed off was on the rise. Not all secular ideas are wrong, of course, and perhaps it is true that these religious values are best left for education at home rather than in school—most of my fellow millennials didn't receive them in either—but when we remember that it was religion that first gave us literacy and education, we can think twice before pushing its moral values away from the world of academia.

It was John Paul II who said:

> *Faith and reason are like two wings on which the human spirit rises to the contemplation of truth; and God has placed in the human heart a desire to know the truth—in a word, to know himself—so that, by knowing and loving God, men and women may also come to the fullness of truth about themselves.*[2]

---

2. John Paul II, *Fides et Ratio*, epigraph.

The Artist

WHEN I WAS AROUND twelve years old, I got "possessed" by the drive that takes over early teenagers. . . no, not that one, the other one. The need for great music. . . and the need to build an identity around a particular genre.

It's funny how, for many people, until we reach a certain age, music is nothing more than a nice enough combination of sounds. It's something that belongs in the background of childhood parties or boring adult conversations, and when people start singing in movies, it is time to yawn. Then we reach a certain age, and something shifts inside. We begin craving deeper meaning, for sounds and lyrics with the power to break our hearts.

My musical journey started by "stealing" my dad's CDs (thank God for his taste). I would take his copy of "Remember the Titans—Soundtrack" and put it on his Walkman CD player, stuff it inside my backpack, and walk to school. I'm not that old, mind you; Walkman CD players were already outdated at the time, hence the hiding-in-the-backpack method. I made sure only the earphones were visible so that other kids would think that I had an MP3 player in the backpack just like them. (I realize now that at the time you are reading this, an MP3 player probably sounds just as old.)

Eventually, I jumped ahead a few more musical decades and got into bands like the Red Hot Chili Peppers and Green Day (my first favorite bands!). By then, I begged my parents for an iPod, just as all the other millennial kids did at the time.

By the time I reached middle school, music was all I thought about for most of the day. I started diving more into my dad's old-school bands. I felt like Luke, learning the ways of the Force from Master Yoda, as he instructed me in the ways of rock and roll with his "Best of the 70s and 80s" DVDs. I have fond memories of my aunt and cousins visiting us from the States. We would spend entire evenings watching those DVDs. My cousins and I watched and learned as my dad and his sister Elizabeth would sing along to Shocking Blue, Yes, Wham, Creedence, The Eagles, The Beatles, Deep Purple, and Jimi Hendrix.

My indoctrination into the world of long hair and guitars was complete, and for the next decade, I spent most of my time writing songs in the middle of classes (in middle school, high school, and eventually university), forming bands with my friends, watching them dissolve, starting new ones, beginning duo projects, solo projects, trying to record in a studio, trying to perform live at events, filming music videos, writing, and collaborating with musicians from different countries, and flying to those countries to play with them live and even sometimes act as their assistant and manager.

During all those years, I always maintained a strict self-made philosophy about music, and I stuck to it religiously: music theory is the enemy of rock and roll. Learning about patterns that work, such as chord progressions, harmony, the circle of fifths, and even scales, is a complete waste of time, and making music with those patterns is the antithesis of rock since rock is about rebelling against rules and the establishment. "How can I compose freely and creatively and make something new if I'm sticking to pre-made patterns?" I thought.

Music was pure magic to me, and music theory seemed like science, or worse, even math.

Years later, I had the opportunity to have a conversation[1] with one of my favorite minds from the 21st century: Professor Warren Smith, a university teacher who went viral in the media after he applied critical thinking to defend J.K. Rowling—the author loved by us millennials for writing Harry Potter—from those who call her a "transphobe."

Warren taught me how patterns and rules can sometimes add to the mystical side of art rather than take from it. He, for instance, used to despise the "Hero's Journey," which is a narrative pattern or template often used as a guide to craft the plot of novels, movies, TV series, and all sorts of stories. The Hero's Journey is often used by religion critics to point out similarities between "man-made stories" and those we call sacred. They also call it the "monomyth." This idea is often criticized as an oversimplification, and fairly so, but could it also be the other way around? Could it be religion and its universal truths that inspired the narrative pattern that works so efficiently in our modern fiction? Could there be something primordial and arcane in the Hero's Journey circle that makes it resonate so well within us? My friend Warren seems to think so, and I think J.R.R. Tolkien—my favorite author—would agree. Upon reading some of his works, like "*Mythopoeia*" and "*On Fairy Stories*," one can infer that Professor Tolkien deeply believed that storytelling is the most powerful of all art forms because of its capacity to transmit Universal Truths.

Perhaps Tolkien is right, and storytelling is the art best suited to pass on our sacred knowledge from generation to generation; it certainly is the most direct and effective one when doing so, but I have seen that all the great arts, when done right, end up being like a giant sculpture that reaches out to the heavens, trying to touch the Divine.

Let us talk about art as a whole, then. Let us ask the questions: Where does art come from? And what inspires great art?

When we talk about the greatest works of art in music, painting, sculpture, and architecture, it is irrevocably true to state that

1. Smith, "Finding the Divine."

many of them are inherently religious and spiritual works; those that aren't are still—most of them—made by deeply religious or spiritual people, from devout Catholics, Orthodox, and Lutherans to mystics and Freemasons.

It is impossible to talk about painting without thinking of "The Creation of Adam" by Michelangelo or "The Last Supper" by Leonardo da Vinci. Other great masters like Raphael, Botticelli, Johannes Vermeer, Diego Velázquez, Paul Cézanne, Rembrandt, and Salvador Dalí were all spiritual people in their way; even if they weren't all "churchgoers," they were as far from being atheists as they were from being internet influencers.

Talk about music, and you will see a similar pattern. Not only were the great masters such as Bach, Mozart, and Beethoven deeply spiritual, but the very foundation of Western music theory was single-handedly developed by religious tradition. From the early notation systems developed in the 9th century with Gregorian chants to Guido of Arezzo's four-line staff notation, and from the concepts of polyphony and harmony, discovered by monks experimenting in Notre Dame Cathedral in the 12th and 13th centuries, to the creation of modes and scales established by the medieval church, all done with a simple goal in mind: to connect man with its creator.

When we talk about the more contemporary arts, I like to look at storytelling. This art adapted perfectly to modern life and technology. Good stories find their way to us, whether through books, films, or even video games. Remember what I told you about Tolkien and the use of stories to pass on universal truths? Maybe this sounds rather mystical or far-fetched to you, but you don't need to be a theologian or a philosopher to realize that some stories endure for millennia, while others fade away from the bookstores after a few decades, and others don't even last the opening week in the movie theaters.

Usually, the latter are stories made for entertainment only, or in my generation, even stories made to push an agenda that only a small minority of the world's population agrees with. But the former, the stories that last forever, are those that carry a message we deeply resonate with as human beings. It also doesn't take a detective to notice that most of those transcendental stories use a message, a theme, or a pattern that is deeply rooted in or inspired by religion and spirituality.

Take *The Lord of the Rings*—Tolkien's masterpiece—for example, this book series has been attributed as the inspiration for all modern fantasy. Many authors agree that it is one of the greatest works of fiction of all time. Peter Jackson's movie adaptations have a colossal total of seventeen Academy Awards. These stories are deeply inspired by Tolkien's Catholic faith, and in them, we can find theological themes that mirror those of our own world. The same or more can be said for C.S. Lewis's *The Chronicles of Narnia*, which serves as a parallel to draw children to Christianity.

In the world of cinema, there is perhaps no greater iconic story than that of Star Wars. While it is not intentionally a religious work, George Lucas combined the beliefs of all major religions to create "The Force," and the entire plot of Star Wars revolves around the redemption of its villain (Darth Vader, that is, the greatest villain of all time in film history), a theme so Christian that they might as well play these movies to kids in Sunday School.

There are some other great secular works of art, of course—novels and films that deal with more "earthly" themes and teach us perfectly good messages about persistence, chasing dreams, and romance. These are perfectly enjoyable and necessary works of art. But every now and then, a story tries to teach the wrong message.

We millennials see countless examples of this as Hollywood and other storytelling agencies have been infiltrated by the woke agenda and continuously try to push failure after failure in movie theaters. Back on the spiritual topic, occasionally, we get authors trying to teach the atheist message to kids in the form of novels. Some have even gone as far as writing entire book series aimed at serving as direct counterpoints to *The Lord of the Rings* and *The*

Chronicles of Narnia. Why is it then that these stories fail to be even half as influential as the traditional works they aim to replace?

The fact remains that atheist philosophy, as well as "woke" ideologies, have been equally unable to produce a single story that has the power to change and influence the world for generations—a story that transcends the mere role of entertainment and rearranges the consciousness of people.

Is it really then that big of a stretch to conclude that the messages in those stories that transcend and stay with us do so because they are true? Not true in the sense that there were elves, dwarves, and wizards in our past, or that we will be fighting with laser swords in the wars of the future, but that there are forces beyond the physical world at work in us, and that even though we can't understand them fully, we know that they are somehow intertwined with the moral choices of this life. That we are beings who will exist beyond our temporary dwelling on this Earth, and that we exist for a reason, and we live to fulfill a greater purpose.

Let us finally talk about architecture, the world where art meets structure and mathematics.

During my twenties, I had a "distant crush" on this ancient art. I never considered it an option as a career path for me, but I can understand and relate to those who do, and I can't help but befriend some of them; I sense the artistic soul inside architects. It also helps that I have always had a fascination with atmospheric and immersive sensations. What can be more immersive, cozy, and atmospheric than the structures we inhabit? Perhaps only nature.

There has always been debate on whether architecture is an art, a science, or both. The reason I love to discuss architecture in spiritual conversations is that buildings and structures are the most obvious and straightforward indicators of a culture's or civilization's identity and direction. Pick up an architecture book or search on the internet for the greatest structures of mankind, and you will see how, like in music and painting, many of them were built with the desire to link humankind with the divine.

If I gave you a million dollars today and told you to travel the world, you wouldn't be excited about seeing the tall corporate buildings of Houston or Toronto; you would long to visit the ancient pyramids of Giza in Egypt or the ones of the Mayan or Aztec civilizations in Mexico. You would be longing to see the Greek Acropolis, the Parthenon, and the temples of Zeus and Poseidon. In India, you would long to see the Taj Mahal, and in Turkey, the Hagia Sophia, as well as St. Basil's Cathedral in Moscow. As for the Western world, don't even get me started with Saint Peter's Basilica in the Vatican, the Cathedral of Cologne, Westminster Abbey in London, the Cathedral of Prague, and, of course, Notre-Dame in Paris.

The secular world is not without its merits. Sure, the Chrysler Building and other New York skyscrapers are iconic, and I may have a dream to B.A.S.E. jump from the top of the Burj Khalifa in Dubai, but the New World hasn't been able to match the level of beauty and craftsmanship of the Old World in its buildings. Some intellectuals will label this kind of talk as "Golden Age Thinking," which is the idea that a different period in time is always better than our own, but I am not falling for that fallacy in terms of architecture and culture.

For the past hundred years or more, we have raised structures toward the skies, not with the intention to connect with God, not even in scientific endeavors like space exploration, but for the sake of making money and growing our businesses and corporations. It takes only half a brain to go outside and see what the secular pursuit of earthly pleasures has done to the aesthetics of our cities, and if you are really paying attention, you will notice how the other arts have decayed as well. Modern paintings are as plain and as boring as the soulless, minimalistic white-and-grey apartments that the modern housing corporations want us to inhabit. Popular music went from Celine Dion, Michael Jackson, Stevie Wonder, and The Beatles to nonsense rap and repetitive mass-produced pop songs, all written in the shadows by one Max Martin.

Even the youngest of arts, like filmmaking, has suffered as well. Nowadays, we rarely get a masterpiece film like *Titanic*, *Jurassic Park*, *The Matrix*, or *The Lord of the Rings*. The modern world is too busy making empty stories loaded with messages of race, extreme feminism, and pseudoscientific gender theories. When modern filmmakers are not busy making these, they go and destroy the old stories one by one with remakes and reboots, all injected with the same heavy doses of propaganda.

Perhaps we don't have the tangible, material evidence that atheists would require to believe in the existence of God, but we do have physical, visible, tangible, and undeniable proof that faith, religion, and all things spiritual are a force for good in our world; an inexhaustible elixir that nurtures our civilizations and grows them rich in both culture and moral values. We have been arrogant and childish in thinking that we can move forward without it. In our belief that we should only drink small sips from it, our culture has grown anemic and sick. One only needs to go outside and look at the buildings, see our paintings, and listen to our music.

The Aviator

WHEN I WAS ABOUT seventeen years old, out of the blue and for no apparent reason that I can remember, my mom took me to the countryside to experience flying in an ultralight airplane.

This was at a lake famous for being a hotspot for extreme sports, particularly skydiving. During those days, I still had the desire to one day become a "jumper," so I wasn't too enthusiastic about visiting this famous site to engage in an entirely different form of flight; nonetheless, I was mesmerized as soon as we arrived at the airfield.

The vivid green of the grass runway reminded me of the French countryside depicted in World War I films, especially when I looked around and found myself among several small airplanes with fuselages made from simple metallic structures and cloth-like fabric forming their wings. The white-and-orange stripes of the windsock made for a nice sight. The small but elegant restaurant next to the grass runway, filled with pilots in brown leather jackets, contributed to a complete aviation atmosphere ready to welcome me.

My mom paid the fare, and soon enough, I found myself sitting in the right seat of the cockpit of a Quicksilver MXII ultralight. After listening to some safety instructions, we taxied to the runway, throttled up, and took off. I never imagined such a natural feeling of flight.

When you take off in a big airliner (a giant barge, as the famous "Red Baron" called them), you feel a little anxious, knowing that something "unnatural" is going on. Deep inside, you know that fifty thousand kilos of metal lifting off the ground to fly is only possible due to some technological violation of the natural world—a mechanical miracle. But when you take off in a small propeller aircraft, you feel perfectly harmonious with the laws of nature and aerodynamics. It is as if the structure of the airplane was designed by nature, helped only by the small human intervention of an engine and some instruments and gauges—the perfect blend of nature and machine. In a small airplane, you feel absolutely nothing as the wheels lift off the ground; one slight movement of the yoke, and you have become one with the avian wildlife.

Once we were up in the air and at a stable altitude, the pilot let me play with the rudder for a little bit so I could experience moving one of the control surfaces. He then asked if I wanted to try some aerobatics, to which I nervously agreed. He started with some simple maneuvers but kept increasing the difficulty as he saw I was perfectly calm and unafraid, which he must have interpreted as unimpressed. In reality, I was probably too overwhelmed to process what was happening or too intoxicated by the peaceful feeling of the wind on my face to care or notice that we were looping or upside down.

"You want to try skydiving, eh?" he said. "Check this out." He idled the throttle and put the airplane into a dive, pointing straight at the ground. I maintained an inexpressive face, but I was loving the G-forces in my stomach every moment. The flight lasted about 20 minutes, and soon we circled back to land. Afterwards, I learned that the pilot told my mom I had "balls of steel." I crawled out of the cockpit of that airplane as a converted man. And during the entire drive home, I was thinking, "Why learn to jump out of airplanes if you can learn how to fly them?"

From that day on, I had a mission to become a pilot, one way or another. That feeling stayed with me, and when I needed a break from university and its halls infested with socialist and anarchist zombies, I heard again the call of the heavens; so at twenty years old, I took a sabbatical year and enrolled in a flight academy.

It was a strange feeling at first. For twelve long years, I had attended school, but now, for the first time, I was learning something that I loved. It was here that I truly understood that quote often mistakenly attributed to Einstein, "Everyone is a genius, but if you judge a fish by its ability to climb a tree, it will live its whole life believing that it is stupid."

I had always done okay in school, but after my teenage years hit and my musical interests took over, I barely cared enough to strive for anything higher than a passing grade; I only ever excelled in English. In flight school, I wasn't just doing okay; I had pristine grades. My newfound friends studied for three to five hours before a test, while I only skimmed through my notebook for forty minutes. For the first time in my life, others were copying my papers!

I enjoyed ground school[1] well enough. I felt like I had ended up where I was supposed to be. After growing up watching Star Wars religiously with my dad (which is a story about a family of space pilots who meet other pilots, really), I felt right at home.

Aviation, as it turned out, seemed to cover many of my passions in one single bundle. I had always been obsessed with weather. I remember feeling extremely cozy in Isla Mujeres while tracking a hurricane's path on the computer. We monitored it to make sure it didn't get too close to us, as the rain kept pouring outside our windows. Meteorology class in flight academy triggered that feeling in me again. I've always thought that if I were born in the United States, for example, there would be nothing I would like to do more than be a storm chaser.

I also had a hidden passion for the military, as I believe most men do. Leather jackets, dark sunglasses, stripes on your shoulders, and other pilot clichés make a young aspiring pilot feel like

---

1. In aviation training, the building with classrooms where student pilots take their theoretical classes is usually referred to as "ground school," while "flight school" is used more often to refer to the practical portion of training, which is flying with an instructor.

he is in the army, or the air force for that matter, even if he is only flying a beaten-up Cessna. Talking on the radio with lingo like "Alpha," "Bravo," and "Charlie" doesn't hurt either.

It wasn't all roses in ground school, of course. Even surrounded by pilots, I sometimes felt like the odd one out.

Almost everyone you meet in flight school wants to graduate and work in the airline industry; the most "out of the box" they get is wanting to be a cargo pilot or fly rich businessmen in private jets. All of those are great jobs, mind you, and they beat working the 9-to-5 in an office. But I fell in love with flying in an ultralight airplane and read the books of Manfred Von Richthofen (the famous WWI aviator known as "The Red Baron").

I wasn't an adrenaline junkie—maybe only a little bit—but I remembered Richthofen's words all too well: "In going about in such a colossus one has no longer the sensation that one is flying. One is driving."[2] I knew then very clearly that whether I was going to fly airplanes as a career or for pleasure, I wanted to fly small propeller aircraft.

Another aspect of flight academy that was hard to come to terms with was the whole "career" thing. Even today, I have difficulty with the idea of doing a single thing for the rest of my life, given my adventurous and artistic inclinations. But during my training days I read somewhere this quote:

> "There's a big difference between a pilot and an aviator. One is a technician; the other is an artist in love with flight."[3]
> —E.B. Jeppesen

Now that. . . that I could relate to.

My mom has always said, "Everything comes with time," and sure enough, after a few months, it was time to turn ground school into flight school. I packed my bags and joined a couple of my pilot

---

2. Richthofen, *Red Fighter Pilot*, 83.
3. Jeppesen, *Afternoon with "Jepp" and the OX5*, 5.

cadet friends in a house in the countryside near an airfield, where we would be living for the remainder of our training.

Even at that age, I had never experienced living on my own, or with roommates for that matter. Mexico is one of those countries—unlike the USA—where almost all university students live with their parents and don't think about moving out until perhaps marriage. I had never lived with people my age, let alone in a different state far away from my family, but I managed to adapt well for the most part, and I knew that my colleagues shared similar feelings.

I was reasonably nervous on my first day at the airfield. I looked the part, with my white shirt featuring a single stripe on each shoulder, but something told me that five hours in the simulator weren't going to be enough to feel comfortable in a real airplane. I only felt worse when I approached the hangar all suited up and ready to meet my instructor, and another—more experienced—cadet showed up . . .

"You're with Morales?" he asked.

"I think so, yeah," I replied.

"Careful then, he falls asleep!"

I was sweating cold and pacing around. Now that I think about it, that other cadet probably went home laughing. I went through the motions and met the guy. He was an older-looking fellow with quite a few grey hairs and somewhat of a "beer belly," but decent enough and friendly with newcomers, although he liked to swear a lot. We did the preflight checks and walked around the airplane a few times.

During my famous first "walkaround," he showed me the routine I now know by heart: looking around the fuselage, empennage, and wings, making sure everything looked sharp. I learned this calmly enough, as I wasn't sure if we were even going out flying that day or not, but when he asked me to join him in the cockpit, my awkward anxiety returned.

I think most cadet pilots, with their nerves of steel—or youthful audacity—would have just brushed off that comment regarding my instructor's tendency to "sleep on the job." They probably would have just hoped for the best and gone on with it. But I wasn't going to get into the air in a sixty-year-old beaten-up tin can for the first time with a sleepy instructor, so I gathered some courage once I climbed into the cockpit and asked him as politely as one can ask such questions. . . "Is it true you fall asleep while we're flying?"

He looked shocked and embarrassed at the same time, as if he was wondering how I could be so audacious to ask that and where I had gotten that information from in the first place. "Well. . .yes," he said. "But I'm not going to do it on your first day, of course!"

That sounded comforting enough for the time being, so after he showed me how to do an engine check and taxi the airplane to the runway, I throttled up and lifted off the ground for the first time in control of an airplane.

It felt just as natural as my baptism in the air during that ultralight flight years ago. The controls were so simple to me and so natural that it didn't even feel at all like the simulator at ground school; instead, it felt more like flying an airplane in one of my favorite video games. "Don't look at the clock," he said. "How much time do you think has passed since we took off?" "Five minutes?" I replied. He lifted his hand from the clock so I could see. . . "Thirty-five!" Time indeed flies when you are having fun, and when you are. . . well, flying.

I was having such a blast falling in love with every second of being in control of the airplane, but soon my official first flight would take an unexpected turn. Maybe it was the nerves, or that I didn't drink enough liquids on that sunny day, or that I had only a light breakfast, but soon the infamous motion sickness crept in on my first day as a pilot. There are truly few things, as far as vehicle experiences go, as horrible as feeling sick inside a tin can two thousand feet high and a couple dozen miles away from the nearest bathroom. We turned back, of course, but it took us about another thirty minutes to return to the airfield. During all that time, I was feeling like throwing up, fainting, and crying all at once.

I went home feeling defeated and called my mom, almost hoping she would tell me that it was okay if I wanted to quit.

Instead, she encouraged me to buy some motion-sickness pills and try again, trusting that I was paired with Mr. Sleepy Instructor for a reason, which was hard to believe at the time.

I followed her advice and tried again after a couple of days of rest. The next time I showed up at the airfield, I met an entirely different version of my instructor. My first flight had turned into a bad experience, and my visible disappointment must have triggered a "dad instinct" in him because he softened up quite a lot and even stopped cursing for a long while!

I got to see a different side of him that I bet hardly any other cadet pilot had seen before me. He reassured me that I could do it and that it was just like in the video games—"but you only have one life," he said—and soon enough, we were up in the air again, time after time; we actually bonded quite well.

In the end, Mom was right again. It turned out that he wasn't into airliners and big jets either. He spent his childhood obsessed with treasure hunting and adventure, and after getting his pilot's license, he flew several missions in the Amazon looking for gold!

He also taught me how to fly by heart rather than exclusively by numbers. He was the only instructor from my school at that airfield who flew and taught in such a way, as I later found out when I had the chance to fly with a few other instructors. I never enjoyed flying with those who kept the checklist in their hands the entire flight and expected you to execute every turn, climb, and descent at the exact airspeed in the pilot's operating handbook.

Once I got over my initial bad experience, and with the help of motion sickness pills for a few weeks, I turned out to be quite the natural. It took me a single lesson to learn new maneuvers, and soon enough, I was signed off as "ready to solo" earlier than the average cadet.

I was having fun again, and so were my friends, living in our own little house and flying every day. Sometimes the feeling turned a little bittersweet and occasionally lonely. We were all far away from our families, and both of my colleagues had recently broken up with their girlfriends. "I have everything I ever dreamed of. . . so why am I feeling sad?" said one of them as we were unsuccessfully attempting to enjoy the pool next to our house on a quiet and lonely afternoon.

I know now the words of Christopher McCandless were true: "Happiness only real when shared."[4]

Flying and learning to fly turned out to be quite a spiritual experience, at least for me. I was surprised by how many spiritual people I met—and continue to meet—while breaking bread with fellow aviators.

It is impossible, of course, that an entire group of people is one way or the other, but the old expression "There are no atheists in the trenches" often came to mind. It seems that the great majority of people who engage in high-risk activities do so partly because they feel protected by a greater force.

This is incredibly funny if you have ever seen one of the psychometric evaluations that pilots undergo. They are filled with questions like: "Do you believe in ghosts?", "Do you believe there's something protecting you?", or "Do you hear voices?" There are many other questions like these meant to check your sanity, but they would also make a theologian raise an eyebrow or two.

I can honestly say that I never felt as close to God in my youth as I did while going through flight training.

I found myself praying constantly in my head during the first several dozen hours in the air. It felt like meditating, and one truly feels closer to the divine while flying. It is not because I think Heaven is in the clouds or God is floating somewhere in space, as some atheists with a poor theological understanding think we do. There is something primordially spiritual about displacing oneself through the air, breaking the normal human routine, and risking one's life that truly makes us feel closer to God when flying.

On the morning of my first solo, I went to the airport with a fighter pilot mindset. My instructor had already vouched for me to fly

---

4. Krakauer, *Hacia Rutas Salvajes*, 151.

alone for the first time two or three lessons ago, so I was well aware that the time for my first solo was approaching.

I flew a short circuit pattern (flying a square around the airport) with my instructor; he then told me to land, after which he got out of the airplane and told me to "go for it." I took a few minutes to collect myself. I called my mom to wish me luck and send some prayers my way. I ran my preflight checks, and I taxied the airplane to the holding point before the runway.

I reached the holding point and joined the line-up in formation with two or three other planes from my school. When it was my turn to line up for takeoff on the runway, I called the tower:

"Cuernavaca Tower, Kilo-Victor-Mike holding short of runway 20, ready. For information: first solo."

As the tower called back on the radio to give me takeoff clearance, I looked over at the plane lined up next to me. The pilot, another student from my academy—already with a couple of bars on his shoulders—was also hearing me on the radio. He gave me a nod and a captain-like gesture with his hand as if to say, "You got this." And I gestured back: "Alright!"

The whole thing looked and felt like a scene from an aviation movie.

"Kilo-Victor-Mike cleared for takeoff on runway 20." I throttled up and gently lifted myself from the earth towards the heavens.

There is no greater flight in a pilot's life than their first solo. Out of all career choices, no first project of an architect, first restaurant of a chef, or first brain surgery can match the feeling of earning your wings. To be the only soul on board and in control of an aircraft, to soar alone among clouds and birds, and finally to return to earth and gently touch the runway with your wheels unassisted.

After I landed, I was ecstatic. I felt like I was living the best day of my life so far. But soon after I left the apron and started walking towards the hangars, as the excitement wore off, my philosophical mind started playing tricks on me.

"What if this is the peak level of happiness, as good as it gets? And now it's over and done." I felt for an instant above the rest of humanity—literally flying in the air—and metaphorically, having experienced something very few people ever get to do.

"What if this is all there is, and God and all the spirits are just inventions of common folk in an attempt to experience a feeling as great as this?" These thoughts swarmed my mind, and the feeling of ecstasy soon turned into a feeling of dread.

I felt just like my bittersweet aviator friends waiting for me back home, happy for achieving their dream, yet their dream lacked meaning without their girlfriends around to share it with.

I had taken God out of the equation, if only for a moment, and my great achievement had become meaningless.

This simple realization made my faith come back rather quickly. It's a bit of a combination of logic and philosophy: if taking away something from an experience makes the experience meaningless (or less meaningful), how can that something not be real?

I spent another month or two practicing flying solo. I trained in cross-country flying and traversed the skies of Puebla, guided only by the "Pico de Orizaba," the highest volcano in North America. I flew towards the state of Guerrero and felt captivated by the green landscape, lagoons, and rivers. Other times, when I was alone up there, I chose to simply enjoy soaring above the majestic town of Taxco, a town of white-and-crimson houses perched on a hill surrounded by tall mountains and waterfalls. After around 12 weeks of adventure, I graduated from flight academy and got my pilot's license.

Even though I had only single and double digits in the hours of my logbook, I made sure to log a variety of different airplanes, models, and sketchy airfields that other student pilots don't often experience on their way to becoming captains of the giant airliners.

I also took the time to travel to Florida for a week and do a license conversion to the American standards; there, I had some of my proudest moments as a new pilot. There was no one to hold my hand there, and after a single checkride with an instructor, I was handed the keys to an airplane like a box of cookies.

The United States of America truly is a great place for general aviation. I had only a hundred hours in my logbook, coming from smaller airfields in Mexico, where everyone thinks twice before handing you the keys to their plane; now I was flying solo in Daytona Beach, following the coast of Florida north and south, and flying in busy airspace next to NASA's rocket launch sites.

Later, life would take me back to Europe after more than a decade since I visited as a child with my mom and dad. There, I would rekindle my love for ultralights, flying the Land Africa, the only Portuguese-manufactured aircraft.

To tell you the truth, even if flying has always made me feel ecstatic and full of joy, sometimes I didn't feel much different than my melodramatic pilot colleagues back in training.

During my first years as a pilot, I hardly had anyone to share my joy with, other than my mother, of course, who would often drive me to the airfield and wait for me in the cozy restaurant by the ramp, next to the parked airplanes. — Why do general aviation airfields always have such cozy, warm, and atmospheric restaurants, by the way? I will never know—but I really didn't have many friends to talk to at the time, much less a significant other.

The wounds of a past relationship were still lingering, perhaps, and as for friendships, as a young millennial, I fooled myself into thinking that I could satisfy those needs with live streamers on the internet and their followers, which would backfire on me sooner rather than later.

During my first years as an aviator, I noticed a trend among my co-pilots and instructors of wearing a thin rope bracelet with an anchor on it. I never found a clear explanation; perhaps it is just the "captaincy" symbolism of the anchor, combined with the love of ships and sailing that many of us pilots have.

My mom had a different idea, though: that it served as a reminder to stay safe and "anchored" to the ground. When I think about it, some of my happiest moments in the air were when I also had someone or something to look forward to waiting for me after I landed. I had earned my wings, and now I was on a mission to find my anchor at all costs, even if I had to search all around the globe for it.

What is distance to an aviator anyway? Only a minor obstacle that yields to the powers of time and speed.

The Soulmate

I HAVE BEEN PONDERING whether it is appropriate or even storytelling-worthy to share my quest for true love, which involves a lot of texting, video calling, online dating, and other modern practices often left out of respectable romance novels.

I changed my mind recently while on a night drive back from an aerobatics show in Lisbon. I was playing Green Day, Avril Lavigne, and other early 2000s hits on the car's speakers when I thought to myself, What the hell, this is a book about millennials; let them hear tales of finding love on the internet.

However, in order to keep the story more romantic—and to protect myself from a potential lawsuit—I'm going to replace the names of real people with names of celestial bodies. Quite the poetic experiment, right?

Lyra

With everything I have told you about my life to this point, you probably figured out that I have always been what some call a "hopeless romantic."

Perhaps you are still wondering what happened to that island crush, Lyra.

Naturally, when I was old enough (around high school age), I tried to find her. It turns out that in that quest, I ended up finding my whole group of friends from the island. They all stayed in touch with each other after elementary school, and it felt like I was the missing piece. They invited me to their group chats, and we spent hours catching up on the last ten years or so.

I bet millennials were the first generation to easily reconnect with cross-country childhood friends online.

After what felt like several weeks or months of planning, my mom and I took a plane to Cancún to fulfill what felt like a long-overdue visit. I was determined to see my millennial childhood friends again.

Sofía was the kindest. She picked me up from the airport and gave me a tour of Isla Mujeres, where I saw how much it had changed—and how much still felt the same—in the time I was away. I hadn't visited a single time in over a decade since I left, if you can believe that.

We drove around the island, and she took me to see the little yellow-painted school where we all met for the first time as children. What a nostalgia trip! We met up briefly with other ex-classmates who were a little less excited about seeing me (I wasn't a bully, but sometimes we carried the jokes a little too far as kids, I'm afraid), and we finished the day eating ice cream at sunset next to the Caribbean Sea.

After sundown, I headed back to the mainland to meet up with Lyra the next day as I had planned. Sofia wished me luck almost sarcastically, as she knew what to expect from her better than me.

Lyra had, in fact, not replied to my messages at all since I landed in the same state as her. The night before we were supposed to meet, I must have sent her a long and outraged message about how disappointed I was to have traveled all the way there for nothing, because she ended up replying with an apology and an invitation to meet up, with her home address attached.

The next day, I took a cab, which drove me to her elegantly gated neighborhood. I could tell I was in the right place because the security guards asked me for her name to let me through. I stepped off the cab and nervously walked towards the doorbell to ring it, just as I must have done a decade ago in her island home before our first date, releasing turtles into the sea. I waited, called, and texted, but no one answered. That was the day I learned that my so-called "first love" wasn't my soulmate.

Maia

Transitioning from middle school to high school was a tough process for me, not only because my middle school was private and high school was public, but also because all my friends went to a different high school specializing in engineering, while I took a different path, looking for art-oriented classes. These were my close friends with whom I had started my short-lived musician career, my teenage best friends. I visited them often in their new school, where I met Maia.

Talk about millennial good taste; Maia introduced me to great music at the time. She was more into darker-sounding bands like My Chemical Romance and cult-classic TV shows from the 90s like *The X-Files*.

As luck would have it, she lived in a small town about two hours by bus from Mexico City. I gladly made the trip many times, and perhaps my favorite part was that I could stay over at my bandmate's house—who lived close by—write new songs, and rehearse our music after paying her a visit.

That whole thing lasted about a year or so. We were only eighteen at the time and didn't know how to deal with relationship problems. Her mom fell really sick at the time, and that only made the tension higher, as I didn't know how to help her deal with such hardships, even after having experienced losing my own father to the same illness.

I knew our relationship was over when I performed a show at my high school, where I was supposed to dedicate a song to her at the end of the setlist, but she didn't show up at all. I let the public know, though. It made for a very emotional performance and made some girls in the crowd swoon.

That relationship meant enough to me that it made me not want to date anyone for a good six or seven years. I promised myself that I wasn't going to get my heart broken ever again, even if it meant staying single until I knew for sure that I had found the one. I would, of course, fail at this task at least a couple more times.

Astranna

Many years followed, and in the loneliness of my university years (and after taking a break to become a pilot), I decided to make an account on a Catholic dating app. I figured looking for someone who shared my spiritual orientations would get me closer to finding my long-awaited soulmate, and the religious nature of a dating website definitely helps filter out the type of "party girls" that I wasn't interested in.

After flying back to my childhood island and riding 2-hour buses to meet a girl, I had quite honestly acquired a taste for the idea of long-distance relationships.

What is not to like? If you are a hopeless romantic, you dream of going through great deeds and trials to prove your love to your significant other. You look forward to the bittersweetness of airport goodbyes and the moment when you and your lover leave each other's arms. You can practically see yourself in slow motion as you walk near the airport gates, each leading to the inside of an airliner bound far away to different parts of the Earth. You quietly enjoy the guilty pleasure of listening to melancholic songs as you look through the airplane window. Your life is now turned into a scene ten times better than what any blockbuster romantic film could aspire to. What is not to love about that?

It was precisely this philosophy that made me tick the box saying "open to meet people from anywhere in the world," both literally in the dating apps and metaphorically in my mind.

That is how I came to meet Astranna. An animation student from the eastern United States. Astranna was a very kind and polite girl with a great sense of humor and quite a talent for visual art: drawing, painting, and designing.

Talk about millennial relationships! The whole thing lasted about three months. We never got to meet in person, but we got to hang out "virtually" by calling on Skype and playing a few online games together.

We first talked a bit in the dating app, then exchanged phone numbers. One day, I sent flowers to her college campus through one of those website-based services and asked if she wanted to be "boyfriend and girlfriend," to which she replied, "It would be an honor."

I will never forget that elegant gesture. It is indeed very touching when someone sees the value in you that others miss completely, to the point where they consider it an honor to even just hang out with you. Sadly, I will also never forget how her family was a lot less enthusiastic about her talking to a Mexican!

It is funny what some people from the developed countries think of those of us who committed the grave crime of being born in Latin America. It doesn't matter if you are a university student who speaks three languages, has a pilot license, and has a fairer complexion passed down from the French-Spanish genes found in the northern Mexican state of Jalisco. Some people hear "Mexican," and all they see is a fellow with a sombrero picking beans from the ground, trying to steal a "green card" from their daughter.

The day she finally broke up with me, she wrote me a sweet farewell email quoting our favorite authors and movies. Somewhere in there, she wrote that God had a plan for me, which pissed me off a bit because it wasn't God breaking us up . . . it was her and her parents.

In those days, I was at my first peak as a songwriter and at a peak in influence and connections with international musicians as well. I had no better way to let my feelings out, so I grabbed my guitar and a notebook, and for the first time in my life, I felt what the great songwriters describe as "a song that writes itself."

Oh Astranna

I heard it's getting cold there in Indiana

Oh Astranna

Meet me halfway there in Louisiana

Hmm

Hmm

You left me there, stranded at sea

With nothing left but a rosary

You say God has a plan for me

Well I believe in God

But not in destiny

So, Astranna

Meet me halfway there in Louisiana

So, Astranna

Are you getting cold there in Indiana

Are you getting cold there in Indiana

With Astranna I experienced, if briefly, what it's like to be with someone who shared most of my worldviews and values, but I was still missing someone who, on top of the spiritual connection, also shared my sensibility, my art, and my thirst for adventure. . . A true soulmate.

I wouldn't have been able to spend all my days in the same piece of American land without experiencing and bonding with other cultures and seeking exotic sights. That's what would have awaited me, after all, had I stayed with Astranna.

Cassiopeia

When Astranna left me, I gave up the idea of finding someone who matched and fit me perfectly like a piece in the puzzle of my being. "Maybe I'm too picky," I thought.

"And I don't want to spend the rest of my life alone." So I lowered my guard and momentarily forfeited some of my values and promises I had made to myself about how "the right girl for me" should be.

In the autumn months of 2019, I flew to San Diego, California, to perform with Resurrection Fern, one of my musician friends, at the TwitchCon convention. I had a couple of connecting flights, and I ran through the airports and waiting lines and made it just in time to climb up on the stage with her and perform "Astranna" in a heartfelt duet. The stage was set on a rooftop under the afternoon sun, in the autumn Californian breeze. That remains one of my favorite live performances I have ever done.

This was a convention of "live streamers," you see. We millennials were born at a really good time to be musicians, all things considered.

In the past, if you wanted to make a living out of music, you would have needed to be one of the lucky 1% of people to drink from the glorious chalice of fame. Perhaps if you were more into classical music, educated, and connected, you could also make a living well enough in an international philharmonic or orchestra.

Millennial musicians would attempt something never done before: Plug your camera into your computer, and your guitar and microphone into your small mixer, and hit the "go live" button to perform an international concert from your bedroom.

YouTube musicians existed already (another frontier conquered by millennials). People like Lindsey Stirling, The Piano Guys, and Peter Hollens found international fame uploading their music videos to YouTube and growing an audience so big that soon they found themselves doing world tours.

But these YouTube musicians were still somehow "one percenters." Live-streaming musicians had something that they didn't: a small but loyal fanbase committed to watching them 3-4 times per week, paying a monthly subscription, and occasionally spending a little extra cash every now and then to request a song to be added to the setlist. If you played your cards right in those days, with only 50 to 150 concurrent virtual spectators, or "viewers," you could easily make enough money to quit your day job. A new era of musicians was born.

With my talent for networking and connecting with artists, I had soon befriended more than a dozen of them. These conventions were great to meet some of your idols and "online pals" in person for the first time. That year in San Diego, after a couple of years of virtual friendship, I met Cassiopeia.

In the midst of all the excitement of being around semifamous musicians, performing live, and dining with them, I found myself dating one of my favorite singers.

I was no stranger to long-distance relationships, as you know, so after we made our feelings known, I found myself traveling back and forth to Atlanta for what became my first serious relationship since Maia—a relationship I allowed to last longer than it should have.

Here we arrive at the dark side of meeting people on the internet. The truth is that no matter how many live streams you watch, how many video calls and gaming nights you share, you never truly know someone until you "break bread" in their home and meet their family, which is quite a gamble in a long-distance relationship.

I always knew Cass to be a "Christian." Even if she was "from a different church," I thought we had enough beliefs in common based on what I gathered from listening to her songs and watching her livestreams. The truth is that she only shared small bits and pieces of her beliefs that she knew wouldn't sound weird to anyone. Even if some of our mutual friends knew a thing or two about her "church," we had no idea it was founded in the eighties by a guy from Ohio who claimed to have heard God's voice and who later died of ocular cancer after years of preaching while staring straight into the lights. Little did we know that her church's second president ordered his followers to burn books and train with firearms. Little did we know about her church's cult-like behaviors, such as "love bombing" new members or "mark and avoid" those who leave. The truth is that the United States is quite a long way from Jerusalem, and many Americans sadly have no clue what authentic Christianity is supposed to look like. I will give you a clue: a megachurch ain't it.

Put yourself in my shoes now, if you would be so kind as to humor me . . . Imagine you are in an entirely different country, meeting the relatives of your date, and they take you to a country house on the outskirts of rural Georgia for a "Bible fellowship."

"I like going to church," I thought. "This can't be much different."

It started as a friendly enough Bible reading gathering, but soon each person in the group took turns, and when the leader commanded them, each started babbling nonsense, claiming they were "speaking the tongue of angels."

I was a very passive Christian at the time, but I remembered from Sunday school that "speaking in tongues" meant that the Apostles could evangelize in their mother tongue around the world, and yet people in the crowds from different regions were able to understand them.

I found myself a couple thousand kilometers from home, in the middle of a fundamentalist, Pentecostal, pseudo-Christian sect bordering on a cult.

I felt deeply alone in that relationship. She made me promise not to talk to anyone about her beliefs (because deep down she knew how they would look to outsiders), so for a long time, I had nobody to comfort me or validate my suspicions.

I put on a mask and made occasional guest appearances in her musical live streams. I knew that nobody watching me had the slightest idea what I was going through. In fact, I believe most people watching were men who wished they were in my shoes. Be careful what you wish for!

Since Astranna left me out for the sharks, I had given up on the idea of "finding the one," so I spent the better part of two years just trying to find peace and a middle ground with Cass.

She didn't care for any middle ground, though; she wanted someone fully committed to her church, and she hated my Catholicism, even taking offense at it.

Christians have prayed for the heavenly intercession of their departed loved ones for two millennia, but when she caught me asking for my dad's prayers, she thought I was talking with demons!

There were some great times and fun memories shared with Cass, of course. We showed each other some of our favorite spots in our countries, kept each other company, and tried to help each other with our respective dreams and goals. But little by little, the voice in my ear that knew I wasn't going to be happy in a cult kept getting louder, and soon something would change that reminded me what I was really looking for. This is when I came to a breaking point that people reach at one moment or another in their love lives . . . When we ask ourselves that question from the lyrics of that iconic British punk band: Should I stay or should I go?

Luna

I was already getting into the mindset of leaving that relationship, but I probably would have procrastinated on it a while longer if I hadn't been rescued by Luna.

God works in mysterious ways, they say. It wasn't so mysterious to me when a girl messaged me asking for the chords to my song "Astranna." I always wrote music as a way of sending out a "message in a bottle" to be cast into the ocean, hoping for a rightful lover to come to my rescue. Luna listened. . . and rescue came to me from across the Atlantic Ocean.

It's funny how some girls are. They all love to watch romantic comedies, half of which have plots about a boy or a girl in a mediocre relationship who then meets the right person and must choose between the two. They all cry happy tears in the end. . . but watch them raise hell if they find themselves in that same position in real life, when it is their turn to be in the shoes of the losing party.

I faced hell when I broke up with Cassiopeia, both from her and from her girlfriends—those friends who were either too blinded by friendship or too ignorant and uneducated to distinguish a proper Christian of any denomination from a televangelist.

But I have never cheated in my life. I ended that relationship with no idea what was going to become of me in the future, but I had the strength to do so because of the new friend I had found.

Luna and I talked as friends for some months. We shared our favorite music with each other and even exchanged our original songs. It is worth mentioning at this point that Luna is a talented pianist and composer. She also enjoyed listening to the small radio show I was hosting at the time, where we loved to discuss the meaning of songs and the power of music among friends and my other three or four loyal listeners.

I remember one time when she requested that I play a song in my show called "Guardian" by Lindsey Stirling. She told us how the young violinist from California wrote this song as a reminder of how our departed loved ones "watch over us as guardians."

I could tell right away that we were both on the same page spiritually, philosophically, musically, and artistically.

I felt something then that I hadn't felt in years. . . maybe ever. . . And that something made me think, wait a minute. . . There are actually girls out there who appreciate the way I see the world? Girls who value what I believe, who think that the acoustic folk music I play in the car is not boring?

I had, in all honesty, given up all hope of that, and I think many people do as well, looking at the divorce rates of the 21st century.

There is a saying pilots have: "You start with an empty bag of experience and a bag full of luck. The trick is to fill the bag of experience before the bag of luck runs out." I have found that it is similar in relationships; we have to fill our bag of experiences in good relationships before we enter a bad one as adults; otherwise, we may think that a bad relationship is the status quo.

I believe there are thousands of people out there staying in mediocre relationships, even toxic ones, simply because they don't know better.

I knew better; talking with Luna had reminded me of that. So I broke free and jumped into the abyss without knowing what was on the other side.

I was now free to talk to her as a single man. I liked her, sure enough, but I never imagined anything would happen, even with my hopeless romantic nature and my weakness for long-distance relationships. . . She lived across the Atlantic in the Republic of Portugal!

Luna and I finally fell in love by the autumn of 2021.

One piece of advice that everyone gives about starting a long-distance relationship is to meet in person as fast as you can, before doubts and questions start to creep in. But I met Luna right in the middle of the Covid pandemic that peaked for over two years.

I told Luna that I was going to try to visit her by February of that upcoming year, but I did not know in truth when it would be possible. The pandemic had airlines halting flights and airports with extreme restrictions, and Mexico wasn't on the list of allowed visitors in Portugal, but in December of that same year, a window of opportunity appeared.

I found myself visiting my family in Texas to attend my cousin Yasmine's wedding a few weeks before Christmas. Once I was there, I realized that flights to Portugal from the United States were allowed under certain conditions, so I extended my stay a couple more weeks to meet quarantine regulations, and after spending a very Texan Christmas, I bought the first ticket out of Dallas, bound for Lisbon.

After a peaceful layover in New York, I found myself on a night flight crossing the Atlantic Ocean. I slept safe and sound for most of the flight and woke up the next day right on time to see the golden rays of sunrise painting the stratus clouds above the ocean orange.

Minutes later, out of the colossal sea and in between the misty clouds, the European continent emerged; "I missed you" was the first thought in my head, as the memories from visiting Rome, Venice, and Paris with my parents came to mind.

After a swift landing and walking through the Lisbon airport with my heart racing, I found myself for the first time in the arms of my love; her parents were there too, waiting for me. They wanted to make sure their daughter's new boyfriend from across the ocean wasn't some internet creep.

All was well, even in the middle of a worldwide pandemic and having to take Covid tests after a long journey. I was holding the hand of Luna, strolling through the streets of a new country.

It felt just right. It was a day of firsts, and soon enough, after we found ourselves alone in the attic of her home listening to piano music, our first day together turned into our first kiss. I knew the moment our lips touched that she was the one.

"Eight thousand kilometers for a kiss?" I thought, "Worth it."

I spent the next three weeks getting to know Luna better and discovering Portugal. We walked the streets of Lisbon, still adorned with Christmas lights and winter spirit. We sailed the Tagus River and explored the castles and palaces in the homely hills of the town of Sintra.

When it was time to leave, I gave Luna my most valued possession: my silver cross necklace, gifted by my mother and borrowed by my father in times of hardship. I knew that distance was going to be hard for her. To me, the European continent was just one expensive night of sleep away, but for her, having never traveled that far before, the American continent was half a galaxy away. . . but if she had my cross, she would know for certain that we would meet again.

And we did; half a year later, it was her turn to visit me and my family in Mexico. I took her to Taxco, the town I had flown over so many times during training. I took her to see underground cave systems and silver mines to indulge her geologist-adventurer heart. It is fair to say she loved my country. Half a year after that, we couldn't stay separated any longer, so I packed my suitcase along with my dreams and moved to Lisbon.

I guess you could say, if you wanted, that Astranna was right.

That God's plan was for her to come into my life only to serve a utilitarian purpose to make me write a song that would eventually lead me to Luna.

Atheists reading this would love that, so they could accuse me of making up my own meaning and giving credit to an invisible force. While that version of "God's plan" would be poetic justice for me, it is still missing one key ingredient: free will.

My mother always told me that we aren't puppets to a God that moves us through invisible strings that dictate our every action. We were given the gift of free will to make our own choices.

Many who criticize humankind and accuse us of being evil and destructive forget that they are human too and that their very judgment is a testament to a higher morality. These people also miss this concept of free will. Like Agatha Christie once wrote, "*There is too much tendency to attribute to God the evils that man does of his own free will.*"[1]

We humans, as a species, have the God-given capacity to do great good or to do great harm, and it is entirely our choice which path we take. In the same way, we have free will to dictate the course of our lives and to choose the people we want to bond and connect with.

Maybe God has a perfect soulmate waiting for you somewhere out there, but that doesn't mean that you are predestined to be with them or even to find them. You are perfectly capable (with your free will) of missing them entirely by staying all day in your room playing video games or by remaining in your comfort zone, never exploring or traveling. You are perfectly capable of meeting the right person, but staying with the wrong one out of fear of the unknown, for comfort, for lack of an adventurous spirit, or for being a coward.

1. Christie, *Caso de los Anónimos*, 40.

Listen to your heart and your head when making decisions if you want what is best for your soul. If you feel like something is wrong, it probably is. If you are in a relationship and you constantly feel like someone else would treat you or understand you better, even if you have never met someone like that yet, it is still probably true.

You don't have desires for things that don't exist. You don't have needs that can't be met, but we'll talk about that later. . .

My Generation

Perhaps you have heard of another aviator with the heart of a writer who came before me: His name is Antoine de Saint-Exupéry; his masterpiece is *The Little Prince.*

The Little Prince lives on his very own little planet until he sets out to explore the other little planets around him. Each planet is inhabited by a single person who, in turn, represents an archetype of troubled adults that the reader can soon identify in our own world.

If I were the little prince and wanted to show you the types of young adults (and their planets) that I have seen around in my solar system, it would look something like—pardon my dark sense of humor—this:

The depressed man, the anxious man, the woke, and the screen addict.

I have told you stories that happened at the crossroads of two millennia, where the 20th and 21st centuries met. Here, in the timely domains of my generation, I can tell you one thing I have learned about people: those who actively pursue the Divine are the happiest.

Perhaps not everyone will be able to relate to this, but those of us who grew up in healthy religious families notice something different when visiting our friends from school in their secular households. At first, it feels like everyone in the house is a little introverted and quiet, as if lacking a certain "small town warmth," as if lacking a certain joy. It feels like everyone is living just for the sake of being alive. The parents go to work to keep food on the table, and the children go to school to have a bigger table to put food on when they grow up.

Generally, the people who regularly go to church, pray, meditate, and engage in religious rituals (without becoming fanatical) are the happiest, followed by those who are a little more passive but still identify themselves as "spiritual." They still engage in religious communities and spiritual practices from time to time.

Then come those who don't know what to make of the spiritual and don't care enough about it to form an opinion: the self-proclaimed agnostics. Many live normal lives, but this is where you start seeing patterns of anxiety and depression more commonly, only to be surpassed by those who believe there's nothing: the existentialists, the materialists, the nihilists, and the arrogant atheists.

I have seen examples of each of these groups in my social circles. My friend, who—for example—doesn't feel religious at all but nevertheless adheres to religious traditions like "Dia de Muertos" (Day of the Dead) in Mexico, has better mental health than my agnostic friends, most of whom have diagnosed depression and/or anxiety. They, in turn, have better mental health than my atheist friend (a devout existentialist thinker), who at one point became so depressed that he couldn't get out of bed for months.

In contrast, my best friend, who is a physicist and aspiring astrophysicist, has some of the best mental health in my social circles. He has always been somewhat of an "agnostic" too, but he has become more spiritual over time, interestingly enough. He has gone from "I only believe in what I can see and touch" to recently telling me, "Well, science is pretty limited, and it doesn't know everything." The same can be said for my depressed existentialist friend, who was finally able to get out of bed more easily this year after he finally gave up on atheism. Nowadays, he is dating a cheerful Catholic girl who fills his days with happiness.

It is true what Leah Mychal—a well-known Catholic influencer—once told me in a conversation for my podcast: *people get more religious with age, not less.*[1] When we are young, we think that this is because older people are closer to dying, so they want to be prepared for when their time comes, but in reality, it is because experience and wisdom—both of which come with age—enable people to perceive the greater forces at work in our lives more easily.

When you take all of this into account, it is not hard to conclude, if you simply observe the people around you, that life without God is simply meaningless. If you don't believe me, ask those who do not believe in God; the pessimists among them will tell you that life is indeed meaningless, while the optimistic ones will tell you that it is a beautiful thing that life has no meaning.

In my travels and experiences, I have identified what I like to call the three lies of modern society. There are probably many more lies that modern society sells us, of course, but these are the three that I have seen affecting the spirituality of my generation (millennials), the previous generation (Gen X), and the one after us (Gen Z). The three lies that I have observed are as follows:

Something is okay as long as it doesn't hurt anyone

This is the prime example of vague morality. Many evil things can be stopped in their early stages, just like a disease; a disease often appears to be harmless or only hurts a little at the beginning, and similarly, harmful ideologies seem innocent when they start. The most prominent example is, again, gender ideology. Many people in my generation allowed gender ideology to grow and infect the world because they thought, "It's their own business, and they're not hurting anyone." Then, a couple of decades later, we saw gender ideology tear apart everything good that feminists built over the last hundred years. Suddenly, male athletes were allowed to

1. Mychal, "Catholicism and Extraterrestrial Life."

compete against women, forcing them out of their rightful place in the Olympic Games and other sports competitions. Suddenly, men were allowed in spaces where women are vulnerable, and suddenly, parents in progressive countries lost custody of their underage children because they opposed letting them undergo a mutilation surgery that someone else convinced them they needed.

The meaning of life is to be happy

How many times have you heard this? And yet, does it resonate as true deep within your soul?

"If the meaning of life is to be happy, then why don't you go do drugs right now? That will make you happy," argues my friend Professor Warren Smith.

"Well, no, because that would hurt the people who love me," replies the skeptical student.

"Ahh, so then it's not all about your happiness."[2]

This lie is also intertwined with the previous one: *"as long as it doesn't hurt anyone."* If we believe individual happiness is the greatest purpose in life, we may start thinking that it is a horrible thing to interfere with anyone else's happiness. The problem is that, often, things that make an individual happy can be harmful to others, or even to themselves, in the long run. This is obvious to anyone who has children. Sometimes we need to get in the way of other people's happiness for the greater good and often for their own well-being.

It is also important to understand and recognize genuine happiness and joy. I remember taking a philosophy-related class in high school with a teacher who was quite the existentialist—ironically—and he preached the idea that life had no meaning and that the only thing that matters is doing "whatever makes you happy." He told us that he sometimes received very silly answers from students who claimed their only purpose in life was their PlayStation. My existentialist teacher laughed it off and ultimately concluded

2. Smith, "Teacher asks if I believe in God."

that it was a fair answer—and as good a purpose as any—if playing games all day truly makes you happy and gives you a reason to get out of bed in this meaningless existence.

I have met a few people who spend every waking hour in front of a monitor playing games, and let me tell you, that is not happiness; it is a dopamine addiction stemming from the illusion of purpose and achievement that video games provide. Trust me, I am a gamer myself—with moderation—as you probably inferred from some references in my book, but a life where your sole reason for being on this planet is to live in a simulated world isn't a life worth living. Perhaps we have set the bar so low for what a happy life looks like that most of us will settle for anything.

Death is what gives life meaning

This lie is one I particularly despise. How many times have we heard this phrase in a modern Hollywood movie? If you stop for a moment to think about it, it sounds quite "necrocentric." When did we become worshippers of Death, claiming that death is the higher power that grants meaning to our existence? Are we supposed to believe that something is only beautiful or meaningful if it has an end? Really?

Then why do we say things like "I love you forever" or "love never dies"? From the Greeks to the Vikings, from ancient Egypt to the Mayans, from Christians to Arabs, humans crave the infinite. We restore and preserve our greatest works of art. We seek beyond this world and from this life to the next, not as a form of escapism, but as weary travelers looking for a way back home. We seek (once we are mature enough) the love that will remain with us permanently, instead of a fling that lasts only for the summer. Is it not true, then, that it is the eternal things that give meaning to life?

What is it that has been missing inside the hearts of our generations, that some are finally starting to see as the civilization around us crumbles?

A Need for Something Real

"Creatures are not born with desires unless satisfaction for those desires exists."

—C.S. Lewis[1]

IN 2023, I STARTED hosting a talk show in my spare time to have the opportunity to sit down and talk to some of my favorite artistic personalities and share our conversations with the world; one of my favorite conversations was the one I had with Sandra Rudzite. Sandra is a well-known artist from Latvia and an acquaintance of mine for many years. She is famous for her gorgeous dark aesthetic oil paintings that are sometimes inspired by the fictional worlds in video games (I have a pen sketch of hers, which I'm very fond of).

We talked for a couple of hours about music, art, and the human pursuit of beauty and truth. . . You know, everyday conversations for a student of philosophy like Sandra.

I've always known her to be a declared skeptic and an atheist, so I pressed her a little on the topic of religion and spiritual practice towards the end of the episode, and what she said stuck with me for a long time.

"You know, in my skepticism, I keep looking for a similar experience. . . a substitute for what spiritual people have in their

1. Lewis, *Mere Christianity*, 136–37.

lives. I am trying to find that in a secular lifestyle. But I have to say there's always something missing."

She continued, "There is a part that is not engaged. Even if I try to replace spirituality with philosophy, art, etc. There's still something missing."

"But I'm okay with that," she concluded. "I like the mystery."[2]

I didn't have a clever response planned for such insight; I was simply humbled by Sandra's honesty in sharing it with me. I suspect many agnostics and atheists feel the same way, but they might not recognize it, and if they do, many wouldn't want to accept it.

Arrogance, after all, seems to be a defining characteristic of many atheists.

It is extremely hard to find people who understand themselves well enough to tell when something inside them is missing, let alone know what that missing thing might be.

This is the bottom line of why I think so many people from my generation—and the next generation as well—are going through life feeling lost. Because "something" is missing.

I believe that the reason we see an overwhelming amount of mental health issues in millennials and Gen Z (compared to previous generations) can be traced back to two main factors: the lack of a spiritual practice and a code of moral values, along with excessive screen time and smartphone addiction.

I will let people much smarter than me talk about the latter. There is a great book by Jonathan Haidt called *The Anxious Generation*[3], where he exposes how the brains of Gen Z have been "rewired" and permanently damaged by the rise of smartphones, resulting in an increase in mental illness. I would rather address the former reason myself: the lack of a spiritual practice and a moral code or religious values in millennials and Gen Z.

Millennials were raised mostly by Generation X parents. Some would argue that the defining characteristic of Gen X parenting was

2. Rudzite, "Pursuit of Beauty and Truth."
3. Haidt, *The Anxious Generation*.

the desire to break away from the rigid and strict parenting styles of previous generations in favor of a more flexible and encouraging approach. Our parents taught us to chase our dreams and encouraged us to study something we are passionate about in university rather than just pursuing what would make us money. They taught us to drink responsibly and gave us permission to party and come home late. With all those nice perks, though, came some degree of mediocrity and laziness. Think "participation medals for everyone in school competitions," and you get the idea.

Even though most of our parents were raised with fairly open-minded religious foundations, they thought it would be a good idea to let us millennials "decide for ourselves what to believe" and "pick whatever religion or beliefs we want when we grow up." Unfortunately, religion, spirituality, faith, and moral values don't work that way. They are called "foundations" for a reason. Perhaps this is why—like my favorite Latvian painter would say—many of us walk with a "void," or a hole, that very few know how to fill.

A generation that goes about their day-to-day lives thinking that there's no good reason for anything to happen, that their mere existence is only a product of coincidence and random chance, and that nobody or nothing is watching out for them, guiding them, or giving them a greater purpose, that this life and this material world and this decaying body are "all there is" and all they can hope for, is a generation bound to have millions of anxious and—you bet—depressed individuals.

Even worse is when my confused contemporaries, who walk with these metaphorical "voids in their chests," try to fit the wrong things inside them. Things with shapes that don't match the shape of these "holes" and therefore won't fit or fill them.

I have found a hilarious irony in this topic in my life. Atheists think that believers are naive because we believe that there's more to the world than materialism, but there is nothing more naive in the modern world than the atheist utopia.

You see . . . Atheists think that when we get rid of religion, what comes in its place is reason and science. They create these utopian scenarios in their heads with flying cars and renewable energy, where everyone is "free from indoctrination" and "living only for today," whatever that means. The reality is that human beings are religious by nature, so when you take their religion away—much like the golden calf story—the only thing that comes to replace it is yet another religion (I will leave it to you to decide whether or not all of them are equally good) or religion-like cults and cult-like ideologies.

Here is where "woke" culture comes in. When you raise a generation without religious foundations, you throw away thousands of years of well-developed traditions, moral values, theology, philosophy, and a sense of community; you essentially leave that generation vulnerable, and then the wolves come.

Another problem with dismissing thousands of years of moral values is that you are left to start from scratch. Imagine being so upset with airplanes and how they work that you try to reinvent them from the beginning. You start jumping from rooftops with poorly crafted wings attached to your arms. You start pedaling down the hill with a fuselage made of cardboard attached to your bicycle . . . You fall and break an arm, all while a 747 airliner is comically flying at 30,000 feet above your head. This is what millennials and Gen Z look like when they try to reinvent love or challenge the concept of health, coming up with things like polyamorous relationships or the "fat acceptance" movement.

"As long as they're not hurting anyone, then it's fine." This is the extent of morality that my generation grew up with. So if Johnny says that he is a girl, "who am I to contradict him? He isn't hurting anyone; where is the harm if I validate him?" Because remember, we have been brainwashed to think that individual happiness is the greatest pursuit in life, and getting in the way of someone's idea of happiness is unacceptable.

"Where is the harm done?" Perhaps you can ask the hundreds of kids who underwent mutilation surgeries and now regret the whole thing as adults, wishing someone had tried to stop them or suggested therapy instead. Perhaps you can ask the female athletes who were cheated out of their medals and podiums by a man who identifies as a woman; perhaps you can ask the female inmates forced to share a cell with a man for the same reason.

This philosophy has led to underqualified people obtaining jobs where lives are on the line, only getting hired because they belong to a minority group. It has fostered a culture of shaming, firing, and canceling anyone with an opinion different from that of the fascist woke cult.

When nothing is sacred, nothing is profane.

"Human beings are spiritual beings." That is a statement that alludes to the nature of our reality and the existence of our soul. Skeptics will, of course, debate this, but. . . "Human beings are religious beings"—that is simply an anthropological fact.

From the Greeks to the Huns, from the Egyptians to the Aztecs, from the Mayans to the Native Americans, from the Catholics to the Hindus, human beings are religious beings, as much as we are "political animals," as Aristotle said.

New Atheists argue that this is a relic of our past, an outdated and harmful practice that we should abandon. Who would have thought I would live to see the day when they were proven wrong?

When my high school friends asked me during those years to explain the importance of religion, I felt awkward answering. Who would have thought I would live to see the day when my dear Catholic Church was going to be one of the handful of institutions in the world standing in defense of reason and science, standing well above the medical institutions that now claim that the mutilation of sexual organs is an appropriate treatment for children?

Standing well above prestigious universities like Oxford or Harvard, all of which, at the time of writing, call students by their preferred pronouns and defy first-grade biology, claiming that an individual can magically choose whatever gender—perhaps even species?—they wish to identify as.

It reminds me once again of that article "What the Church Has Given the World."[4] "So Catholics have a pretty good relationship with science," I thought, "nice." But who would have guessed that I was going to see a day when religion stood as the last bastion of reason and beauty, a safe haven for common sense?

Religion and spiritual practices teach us important lessons and provide a necessary foundation. . . But are those things we are taught even real? Or just helpful illusions?

One has to wonder how powerful a lie (an illusion) can be against the power of truth. "Truth is like a lion," some say. Like a lion, truth is mighty and powerful; it is like a king. Atheists value truth above all else, regardless of how people and their agendas feel about it. That much they got right.

So if the truth of religious and spiritual people were a lie, how could it inspire such greatness? How come it has raised the most beautiful cathedrals, painted the most beautiful canvases, and sculpted the most exquisite figures?

How has it conjured up nations, set slaves free, fed the poor, and protected the vulnerable? How has it served as the inspiration behind constitutions and laws that form the foundations of our countries and appear in the colors and symbols of our flags? Lies usually die fast. How come faith has endured for thousands of years?

"Okay, so the values it teaches are true. . . but is there *really* a God that loves me? Do I really have a soul? Is there really more than this temporary physical existence?" My skeptical teenage self asks inside me.

I keep going back to the words of my artist friend: *"I keep looking for a substitute for what spiritual people have in their lives. But I have to say there's always something missing."*[5]

Her words resonated deeply within me, as I reflected on them for weeks, even months, until I asked myself . . .

---

4. Pinsent and Holden, *What the Church has given the world*.
5. Rudzite, "Pursuit of Beauty and Truth."

"How can someone have a need for something that doesn't exist?"

We have needs that range from solid objects and physical actions like eating (food), drinking (water), breathing (air), getting vitamins from the sun, and exercising our bodies to those needs that are more "invisible," like love, friendship, being understood, having a community, and seeking adventure (flying an airplane, for example).

How can all our needs be met by things that are real? Is it logical to argue that we have this one need for something imaginary that therefore cannot be met?

"All of your needs can be fulfilled, kid. Oh, except for that one spiritual thing. Ignore that; it's a bug in your system. Here, read some Nietzsche instead."

Or would you rather argue that this need can be satisfied by material things?

"Once science discovers which space rock hit the other in a particular order that started the universe, then your need for meaning will be satisfied! Just don't ask what made the rock move or what existed before them."

"Once we are finally able to upload our consciousness to a computer and live forever through technology, your primitive need for an immortal soul will be no more!"

Once you can honestly recognize the need for the spiritual in your human existence, the most logical and rational conclusion is that spiritual things must exist in order to fulfill that need. Being a skeptic, an atheist, or even a passive agnostic is like practicing some sort of spiritual veganism; you can try to fill your diet with all sorts of supplements and inventions, but in the end, you will always be anemic.

Wiser men than I have reached this conclusion. C.S. Lewis wrote:

> Creatures are not born with desires unless satisfaction
> for those desires exists. A baby feels hunger: well, there
> is such a thing as food. A duckling wants to swim: well,
> there is such a thing as water. Men feel sexual desire:
> well, there is such a thing as sex. If I find in myself a
> desire which no experience in this world can satisfy,
> the most probable explanation is that I was made for
> another world. If none of my earthly pleasures satisfy it,
> that does not prove that the universe is a fraud. Prob-
> ably earthly pleasures were never meant to satisfy it, but
> only to arouse it, to suggest the real thing.[6]

6. Lewis, *Mere Christianity*, 136–37.

.

Epilogue

PERHAPS YOU ARE WONDERING where I stand at the end of this story. At the time of writing, I am a few weeks away from my thirtieth birthday, a milestone that many millennials will reach this year. I am writing these words with my feet still on European soil. As I write, I follow the Conclave in the Vatican on my TV with anticipation and excitement, where the successor to Pope Francis will soon be selected. My eyes and the eyes of the world turn to Rome. What a time to be alive and witness these beautiful rituals and all the colors blending like flowers from the garments of the cardinals, bishops, and archbishops: red, purple, and white-dressed holy men contrast with the white marble, gold, and bronze in Saint Peter's Basilica. Fashion expert and entrepreneur Julia James Davis called this place "the last bastion of beauty in the world." What a visual and spiritual feast; a reminder that things which are beautiful and true permeate the world around us, while ideas that are false, evil, or materialistic turn the world grey and cold. True beauty is not in the eye of the beholder; true beauty is universal, or as Bishop Robert Barron once said, *True beauty rearranges our consciousness.*[1]

As I write this, I am getting ready to say goodbye for now to the Iberian Peninsula. I am sitting here with plane tickets in my pocket and one quest in mind. The next adventure on my horizon is not in the skies but in the turquoise waters of the Caribbean Sea. I

1. Barron, "Christ, Miracle, and the Beauty of the Church," [26:35–27:28].

have felt the call for quite some time to take my beloved Luna there, where this whole story started. There, in the warm sands and calm coasts where I grew up, I will ask for her hand with a special ring that I had made. A pair of golden tree branches meet in an embrace that holds a diamond from the ancient land of Israel. Inside lies an inscription in Latin: *Amor Immortalis Sicut Animae.*

Love is immortal like our souls.

I hope these stories of my adventures and reflections in the 21st century have inspired you. It doesn't really matter if you are a millennial like me, a Gen Z, or from a generation a hundred years from now; the truths of the universe are constant and unchanging, but we humans have a tendency for amnesia. If you, like me, find yourself living in a time when the world around you is committed to forgetting the ancient truths of the spirit, then you are lucky, for you have been born in a time when you can witness these truths proving themselves once again.

Embrace the ancient traditions and rituals that your ancestors lovingly left for you to save your precious time. Step up like the heroes of old, climb the steps to return to your kingdom, and pick up your crown. Become like a king: wise and fair, chivalrous, and honorable. Try commitment instead of living free of promises with your lover like roommates for many years. Get married and do it right. Getting married in a courthouse is a meaningless transaction; getting married in a religious tradition is a sacred ritual. Seek meaning and seek purpose. Have children instead of adopting a new cat every couple of years.

If you have already smelled the scent of the Divine in the world, that is great! But if you don't allow that force to be a part of your life, then it will be hard to harness its power. You will need to draw from it strength, comfort, and all the other antidotes for the depression, anxiety, and meaningless existence of the modern world.

You can take small steps like saying a quick prayer in the morning when you feel grateful for waking up to another day in a wonderful life, and while you're at it, make sure to call things by their rightful name. Thank God, not "the universe." As Fr. Ángel Espinosa would say, "Don't confuse the art with the artist."[2]

Many young people still think that the world around them is trying to indoctrinate them to have kids and a nuclear family with traditional values. Maybe a few hundred years ago it was so, but "growing up" in the 21st century means realizing that we're now being indoctrinated to do the exact opposite.

In our teenage years, we all feel the need to rebel against the status quo, swim against the tide, and walk in the opposite direction of the mindless crowds. Perhaps this is a noble quest. Therefore, let us now be the ones to turn the tide and return the flames of faith and reason back to our civilizations. Let us be rebels by being "old school." Let us be rebels by being moral, by having values, and by reclaiming the arcane wisdom of Christianity.

Let us be rebels by seeking beauty and by living with meaning and purpose.

---

2. Espinosa, "Artista y su Creación."

Bibliography

Barron, Robert, with Jordan B. Peterson, and Mike Schmitz. "Christ, Miracle, and the Beauty of the Church." YouTube video, 17 Feb. 2024. https://www.youtube.com/watch?v=T80qA5efwHs.

Christie, Agatha. *El caso de los anónimos.* Translated by C. Peraire del Molino. Barcelona: Editorial Molino, 1983.

Espinosa, Ángel. "El Artista y su Creación." YouTube video, 12 Apr. 2024. https://www.youtube.com/watch?v=91PeBF9Qj1w.

Haidt, Jonathan. The Anxious Generation: How the Great Rewiring of Childhood Is Causing an Epidemic of Mental Illness. New York: Penguin, 2024.

Jeppesen, E. B. "An Afternoon with "Jepp" and the OX5." *Air Line Pilot*, March 1997.

John Paul II. Fides et Ratio. Encyclical letter, September 14, 1998. Vatican. Accessed September 22, 2025. https://www.vatican.va/content/john-paulii/en/encyclicals/documents/hf_jp-ii_enc_14091998_fides-et-ratio.html.

Krakauer, Jon. Hacia Rutas Salvajes. Translated by Albert Freixa. 1ª ed. Barcelona: Ediciones B, 2008.

Lewis, C. S. Mere Christianity. New York: HarperCollins, 2009.

Mychal, Leah. "Ep 5 – Leah Mychal: Catholicism and Extraterrestrial Life." The Gabster Radio Podcast. Interview by Gabriel Picazo. Spotify audio, 24 Nov. 2023. https://open.spotify.com/episode/0wtpZ9PqHGKGpdktaOWsAO.

Pinsent, Andrew, and Marcus Holden. "What the Church Has Given the World." Catholic Education Resource Center. Reprinted from Catholic Herald, May 6, 2011. Accessed September 22, 2025. https://catholiceducation.org/en/religion-and-philosophy/what-the-church-has-given-the-world.html.

Richthofen, Manfred von. The Red Fighter Pilot. Translated by J. Ellis Barker. New York: R. M. McBride, 1918.

Rudzite, Sandra. "Ep 3 – Sandra Rudzite 'MissCoookiez": The Pursuit of Beauty and Truth." The Gabster Radio Podcast. Interview by Gabriel Picazo. Spotify audio, 17 July 2023. https://open.spotify.com/episode/3qj5HLlSR V2YfatHpy3ubC.

Smith, Warren. "A Teacher Asks if I Believe in God." YouTube video, 19 Feb. 2024. https://www.youtube.com/watch?v=n5SPUTfsPqg.

———. "Ep 8 – Warren Smith: Finding the Divine in Music and Film." The Gabster Radio Podcast. Interview by Gabriel Picazo. YouTube video, 9 Apr. 2024. https://www.youtube.com/watch?v=NY8NIgZqoD8.

www.ingramcontent.com/pod-product-compliance
Lightning Source LLC
LaVergne TN
LVHW021616080426
835510LV00019B/2608